The Medieval World

Law and Punishment
in the Middle Ages

Donna Trembinski

Crabtree Publishing Company

www.crabtreebooks.com

Crabtree Publishing Company

www.crabtreebooks.com

Coordinating editor: Ellen Rodger

Series editor: Carrie Gleason

Project editor: Rachel Eagen

Designer and production coordinator: Rosie Gowsell

Production assistant: Samara Parent

Scanning technician: Arlene Arch-Wilson

Art director: Rob MacGregor

Project development, editing, photo editing, and layout:
First Folio Resource Group, Inc.: Tom Dart, Sarah Gleadow,
Debbie Smith

Photo research: Maria DeCambra

Consultant: Mark Meyerson, University of Toronto

Photographs: Alinari/Art Resource, NY: p. 15 (top); Archivo
Iconografico, S.A./Corbis: p. 11, p. 31 (bottom); Art Archive/
Biblioteca Bertoliana Vicenza/Dagli Orti: p. 29 (top); Art Archive/
Bodleian Library Oxford/Canon Misc 416 folio 1r: title page; Art
Archive/Museo del Prado Madrid/Dagli Orti: p. 30; Art Archive/
Dagli Orti: p. 22 (left); Art Archive/Real biblioteca de lo Escorial/
Dagli Orti: p. 5; Nicolo Orsi Battaglini/Art Resource, NY: p. 22
(right); Bridgeman-Giraudon/Art Resource, NY: p. 9, p. 29
(bottom), p. 31 (top); British Library/Add. 19720 f.80: p. 6; British
Library/Add. 24098 f.22v: p. 14; British Library/Cotton Vitellius
A. XIII f.5: p. 23 (top); British Library/Royal 14. C.VII f.136: p. 23
(bottom); British Library/Royal 20 C. VII f.60: p. 19; British
Library/Royal 20 C. VII f.134v: p. 18 (bottom); British Library/
HIP/The Image Works: p. 16 (bottom), p. 17 (bottom); British
Museum/HIP/The Image Works: p. 17 (top); Castello di Issogne,

Val d'Aosta, Italy/Giraudon/Bridgeman Art Library: p. 12 (left);
Granger Collection, New York: p. 10 (top); Erich Lessing/Art
Resource, NY: p. 7 (top), p. 13, p. 18 (center), p. 24; Mary Evans
Picture Library: cover; Musée Condé, Chantilly/Giraudon/
Bridgeman Art Library: p. 10 (bottom), p. 16 (top); Musée Condé,
Chantilly/Lauros/Giraudon/Bridgeman Art Library: p. 8;
Musées Royaux des Beaux-Arts de Belgique, Brussels/
Giraudon/Bridgeman Art Library: p. 25 (bottom); Palazzo
Pubblico, Siena/Alinari/Bridgeman Art Library: p. 25 (top);
The Pierpont Morgan Library/Art Resource, NY: p. 7 (bottom);
Scala/Art Resource, NY: p. 12 (right); Snark/Art Resource, NY:
p. 15 (bottom), p. 20, p. 28

Map: Samara Parent and Margaret Amy Salter: p. 5

Illustrations: Jeff Crosby: pp. 26–27; Katherine Kantor: flags, title
page (border), copyright page (bottom); Margaret Amy Salter:
borders, gold boxes, title page (illuminated letter), copyright page
(top), contents page (background), p. 4 (timeline), p. 4 (pyramid),
p. 32 (all)

Cover: Many of the practices and traditions of modern court
systems began in the Middle Ages. During that time, law schools,
night watches, and prisons were founded, and people began to
train at schools to be lawyers.

Title page: Around 1087, a scholar named Irnerius began
lecturing about the laws of the ancient Romans in the Italian city
of Bologna. People from all over Europe attended his lectures.
The first medieval law school in western Europe, established by
Irnerius at the university in Bologna, still exists today.

Crabtree Publishing Company

www.crabtreebooks.com   1-800-387-7650

Cataloging-in-Publication Data

Trembinski, Donna, 1974-
  Medieval law and punishment / written by Donna Trembinski.
  p. cm. -- (The medieval world)
  Includes index.
  ISBN-13: 978-0-7787-1360-9 (rlb)
  ISBN-10: 0-7787-1360-1 (rlb)
  ISBN-13: 978-0-7787-1392-0 (pbk)
  ISBN-10: 0-7787-1392-X (pbk)
  1. Justice, Administration of--Europe--History--To 1500--Juvenile
literature. 2. Law, Medieval--Juvenile literature.   I. Title. II. Series:
Medieval worlds series.
KJ945.T74 2005
340.5'5--dc22
                                                2005023003
                                                LC

**Published in
the United States**
PMB 16A
350 Fifth Ave.
Suite 3308
New York, NY
10118

**Published
in Canada**
616 Welland Ave.
St. Catharines
Ontario, Canada
L2M 5V6

**Published in the
United Kingdom**
73 Lime Walk
Headington
Oxford
OX3 7AD
United Kingdom

**Published
in Australia**
386 Mt. Alexander Rd.
Ascot Vale (Melbourne)
VIC 3032

Table of Contents

Early Law

From 100 B.C. to 500 A.D., the Romans ruled western Europe. Their empire, which stretched from North Africa to England, had a strong government and a well-organized system of laws and courts. Together, these protected citizens from outside threats, such as wars and invasions, and from inside threats, such as theft and murder.

After the Roman Empire crumbled, western Europe entered a period known as the Middle Ages, or medieval period. The Middle Ages lasted until 1500. Lords, such as kings and great nobles, controlled large areas of land. They gave smaller sections of their land, called manors, to their most loyal supporters.

The supporters, or vassals, were usually less wealthy nobles. They swore oaths of loyalty to their lords, promising to fight for them in times of war and to help them rule. This exchange of land for military and political services is known as feudalism.

▼ *Most medieval people were peasants. They lived on manors, growing food for themselves and for their lords. In return, the lords promised to protect the peasants from danger.*

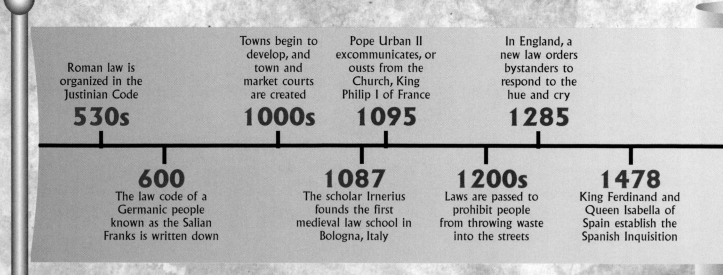

530s
Roman law is organized in the Justinian Code

600
The law code of a Germanic people known as the Salian Franks is written down

1000s
Towns begin to develop, and town and market courts are created

1087
The scholar Irnerius founds the first medieval law school in Bologna, Italy

1095
Pope Urban II excommunicates, or ousts from the Church, King Philip I of France

1200s
Laws are passed to prohibit people from throwing waste into the streets

1285
In England, a new law orders bystanders to respond to the hue and cry

1478
King Ferdinand and Queen Isabella of Spain establish the Spanish Inquisition

▲ Ideas about law in medieval Europe were a mix of Christian rules, laws from the Byzantine Empire, and local ways of settling disputes.

Foundations of Medieval Law

During the Middle Ages, most people followed the religion of **Christianity**. Many medieval laws were based on Christian ideas about right and wrong, while others were influenced by old Roman laws. Still others came from the customs of Germanic people, who migrated into Europe from western Russia in the early Middle Ages.

◀ If a law did not exist for a crime, the Church, kings, and lords made one up. In medieval Europe, laws varied from region to region.

Peasants and Lords

In medieval times, some peasants, called serfs, were tied to the land on which they lived and worked. Serfs could not leave the manor without the lord's permission. Other peasants, called free peasants, enjoyed greater independence.

From Serf to Peasant

Whether people were serfs or free peasants usually depended on the family they were born into. Serfs who wished to be free ran away from the manor to live in a town. Once in town for a year and a day, the serf became free.

Owing Work and Fees

Serfs had to work the lord's land for a certain number of days each year, planting and harvesting crops. They also had to do other types of labor, such as repairing roads and digging wells.

Serfs owed their lord many taxes and fees, which they paid with crops, animals, household goods, or money. The heriot, or death tax, was paid when the head of a peasant household died. A gersum was paid when a peasant rented a new piece of land. Serfs also paid a yearly tax called a tallage. Some of the tallage was used to repair roads, bridges, and buildings on the manor.

▼ *In the fall, peasants in southern Europe harvested grapes and used them to make wine for the lord's feasts.*

◄ *The manor reeve was an official, or representative, of the lord. The reeve collected rent from the peasants who lived on the lord's manor. Peasants paid their rent with money or with crops and livestock.*

Breaking the Law

In exchange for peasants' labor, fees, and taxes, lords and their officials protected peasants from outside attacks and from attacks by other peasants. They also oversaw manor courts, where disputes between peasants, and between peasants and the lord, were heard. In manor courts, peasants sued one another for money they were owed, for items that had been stolen, and for **assaults** they had suffered, both on themselves and on their property.

Serf Versus Lord

Serfs also challenged their lords in courts of law. A serf might appear in court against a lord when the lord demanded work that the serf did not believe they owed him. In one medieval manor court in the village of Elton, England, a lord asked his peasants to move a new **grindstone** to the mill. The villagers argued that moving grindstones was not part of their duties, and challenged their lord to prove his claim in court. He could not, so the peasants were not forced to perform the work. Lords also took peasants to manor courts if the peasants did not do the work or pay the fees they owed.

▼ *Peasants had to pay a tax, called the multure, to grind their wheat and corn into flour at the lord's mill. Those who refused to pay were fined as much as six pennies, which was the same as about 12 days' work.*

Whose Property?

Many laws in towns and in the countryside protected people's property. Property included land, animals, food, and household goods.

Peasants were not allowed to grow food on the lord's land, to collect wood in his forest, or to let their animals graze in his pastures. Anyone who disobeyed these laws was brought before the manor court and fined. Peasants were also fined if they lost or stole other peasants' animals or tools, or if they damaged each other's property.

Theft

Almost half of all recorded crimes in the Middle Ages involved theft. Thieves robbed peasants of their linens, clothing, and cooking utensils, stole vegetables and fruits from private gardens, and even took livestock, such as cows, chickens, and sheep.

The Village Thief

In some cases of theft, people disguised themselves as women or **monks**, people who others usually trusted. The thieves became friendly with the people they hoped to steal from, then robbed them of their money, horses, books, bolts of cloth, or expensive spices. The punishments for theft varied, depending on the value of the object stolen. Usually, thieves were fined. Some thieves who repeatedly stole had an ear cut off as punishment. This warned people who later met the thief that the thief might steal from them, too. If the item stolen was very valuable, such as a horse, a thief was sometimes **banished** from the community, or even **executed**.

▲ *Common land was an area of land shared by everyone. Common land was usually located on the outskirts of a town and on a manor.*

Selling Stolen Goods

Town laws forbade people from selling goods that they knew were stolen. In Paris, France, one shopkeeper was recorded as running a very successful business buying stolen goods and selling them at a higher price. Thieves with items to sell would pass in front of the shop with their fingers on their noses. Seeing this signal, the shopkeeper followed them to an alleyway, where she paid for the stolen items. When city officials discovered the shopkeeper was selling stolen property, she was sentenced to the **pillory** in Paris' main marketplace.

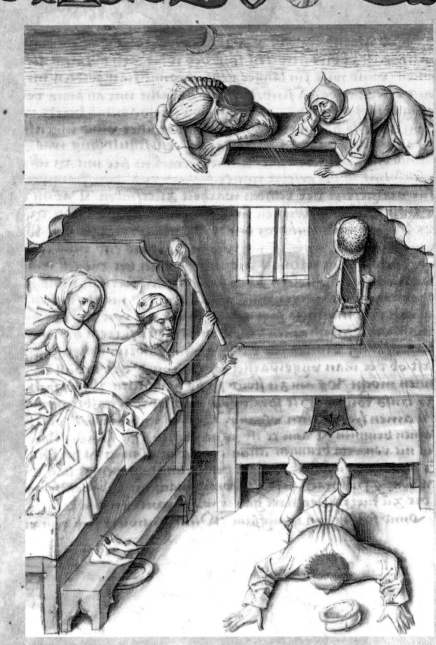

▶ *Thieves sometimes worked in groups of two or three, sneaking into people's houses at night to steal their valuables.*

Robber Barons

Most thieves in the Middle Ages stole because they were poor and needed food and money to survive. Some, such as the English knight John Molyns, robbed for fun. In the 1300s, John terrorized the English county of Bedfordshire. He attacked the **sheriff** and his family, and assaulted the peasants who lived on the sheriff's manor. John stole wool, horses, firewood, and swans, as well as more than 8,000 trees from the king's forests. When John was finally caught, he was declared an **outlaw**.

Who Owns the Land?

Nobles often had disputes among themselves about who owned what parcel of land. Some resolved their disagreements in courts, where they were judged by other vassals of the lord. Others settled their conflicts through trials by combat, in which two nobles **dueled**. The winner was declared the rightful owner of the land.

▶ *To decide on arguments over property, judges examined the properties, questioned witnesses, and studied legal documents before deciding the case.*

The Duel of Engelardus

The French miller Engelardus believed that five mills on the river Seine belonged to him, and that he did not have to pay rent to use them. A group of monks disputed this, saying that Engelardus rented the mills, which rightly belonged to them. Engelardus and the monks agreed to settle the disagreement in a trial by combat.

The monks chose a knight to fight for them, and Engelardus chose his own knight. Armed with shields and wooden sticks, the two warriors fought for an entire day. Engelardus's knight was so badly beaten in the end that he fell to the ground. The monks were judged the rightful owners of the mills, and Engelardus agreed to pay rent for their use.

▶ *For some duels or trials by combat, defendants hired knights to fight for them, instead of doing it themselves.*

Doing Business

After the year 1000, towns in medieval Europe began to develop as centers of trade. Peasants sold their extra vegetables, fruit, wheat, and livestock at town markets.

With the money they earned, peasants bought goods, such as spices and furniture, from merchants and tradespeople. All merchants and tradespeople had to follow certain rules when doing business.

Rules for Tradespeople

Each group of tradespeople had its own laws that limited the number of hours its members could work, set wages for employees, and dictated when shops could open for business. The laws were set and enforced by guilds, which were organizations of people involved in a particular trade. Guild courts were responsible for enforcing a trade's laws. Usually, the punishment for breaking a law was a fine.

In Florence, Italy, the butcher's guild declared that meat from an animal that had died of a disease could not be sold. The guild court appointed inspectors, called rectors, to visit butcher shops once a week to ensure that no one broke this rule. Butchers who sold the meat were fined.

▲ Large cities had many different guilds. There were guilds for butchers, merchants, *blacksmiths*, *barrel makers*, *weapons makers*, *potters*, *and many other tradespeople*.

Laws for Merchants

Laws ensured that merchants measured goods accurately, charged customers a fair price, and sold goods of high quality, such as fresh fruit and thick cloth. If guild inspectors discovered that a merchant had broken a law, the merchant was fined. Merchants who continued to cheat their customers were forbidden to sell goods in the city, and some were banished. People who were banished were forced to leave the city.

▶ *Charters were written laws that guild members wrote describing how their guilds should be governed and what rules their members should follow.*

Markets

To sell their goods at markets, merchants had to obtain a license from the noble who ruled the area. They also had to follow certain laws that were upheld by special market courts. Some laws of markets made sure that families had enough meat, bread, and ale for their daily meals. This meant that merchants sold only to them in the mornings. Then, in the afternoon, extra food and drink was sold to owners of taverns, or inns, or to other merchants. In times of war or **famine**, laws were passed that kept the prices of foods, such as bread and wheat, low. Merchants who did not follow these rules were usually fined by the market court.

◀ *Merchants who sold the same goods had shops on the same street. Vegetable sellers were found on one street, butchers on another, and furniture makers on yet another.*

Fairs

Medieval fairs were large markets held once a year, usually in the summer. Merchants came from all over to trade their goods. To hold a fair, town officials had to get a license from the ruling king or noble. Fairs usually lasted less than two weeks, but they had their own laws and courts.

Keepers of the Fair

People who organized the fair were called Keepers of the Fair. They made sure that merchants sold products of good quality and that they did not cheat their customers. Keepers of the Fair also protected merchants from thieves, and served as judges at special fair courts. People accused of committing crimes at the fair were tried and punished at these courts.

Debt

Most tradespeople and merchants who came before courts of law owed money, or were in debt. The court made the debtor, or the person who owed money, promise to pay back the debt. It also appointed people, called guarantors, to make sure the person paid. Debtors who did not pay were thrown into debtors' prison, until their families or guarantors paid off the debt.

▲ Merchants at medieval fairs traded many different items, including spices, grain, fabric, stockings, jewelry, and copper.

Safe, Clean Towns

Hundreds of laws were passed by governments across medieval Europe to keep towns safe and clean. Anyone who wanted to enter a town had to pass through gates guarded by officials. People suspected of carrying a disease were refused entry. Soldiers or night watchmen protected towns from attack.

Curfews also helped prevent crime. Bells were rung around 9:00 each evening as a signal for taverns and businesses to close, and for house doors to be shut. Anyone caught out after dark by a night watchman was ordered home.

Fire

Fire was a serious danger in medieval cities. Most buildings were made of wood and were constructed close together. Flames from a building on fire quickly spread to other buildings. Whole towns were sometimes destroyed in this way.

Fires were prevented in several ways. Tradespeople whose work involved fire, such as potters and blacksmiths, were not allowed to work in the most populated parts of a city so that they did not endanger the whole city if their fires spread out of control. As well, people were expected to cover cooking fires in their homes when the bells rang for curfew. This cooled the fires or put them out entirely, protecting the city from danger while people slept.

▲ *As people passed through town gates, they often had to pay taxes and tolls. Guards made sure that criminals, outlaws, and other suspicious people were not allowed inside.*

Getting Rid of Waste

In the early Middle Ages, people dumped waste into the streets from their doors and windows, and waited for the rain to wash it away. The result was a very dirty, smelly city. In the 1200s, many towns passed laws that prohibited people from throwing waste into the streets. Medieval houses had to have cesspits, or holes dug into the ground, in which to dump human waste. Town workers emptied the cesspits regularly, carting waste to larger dumpsites or cesspits outside the town gates.

▲ *Many cities passed laws such as when and how butchers could kill cows, to help keep places of work neat and clean.*

Safe Roads

City streets were usually made of dirt and were full of potholes. When it rained, the streets became muddy and slippery. Accidents were frequent, and sometimes resulted in lawsuits between town citizens or between a citizen and the town government.

To make streets safer, many medieval governments paved their roads, but paving was very expensive. In some towns, a person who damaged the pavement during an accident was charged for the repairs. If he did not pay, he was sued in court and fined.

▼ *Streets in medieval towns were filled with people, carts, horses, and other animals.*

Violent Crimes

The most common violent crime in the Middle Ages was physically assaulting another person. This was usually punished by a fine or, in some cases, by a physical punishment.

The Stocks

People who were extremely violent or who committed the same crime several times were sometimes sentenced to the stocks or pillory. Stocks were heavy frames made of wood or iron. They had holes that restrained criminals' ankles as they sat on the ground. Criminals in stocks were unable to move from where they sat. The stocks were set up in public squares, where villagers passing by threw rocks or ripe vegetables at the criminals. Criminals in stocks could defend themselves only by throwing the rocks and vegetables back at those who laughed at them.

▼ Nobles and kings were not usually placed in stocks, but almost anyone else who committed a crime could end up in them, including monks and nuns.

▲ People who were found guilty of moral wrongdoings, such as drunkenness or slander, were sometimes beaten as punishment.

Pillories

Pillories were wooden or metal frames that restrained the head, hands, and sometimes the feet of criminals as they stood. The pillory was a more painful punishment than the stocks because criminals were bound in a hunched-over position for hours or days, at a time. With their hands restrained, criminals could not defend themselves against villagers' attacks.

Being Outlawed

People who committed crimes such as theft and assault were sometimes outlawed. Outlaws were banished, or sent away, from their communities and lost all their legal rights. Anyone could steal their property, or even kill them, without being punished. Towns that protected outlaws sometimes had their walls destroyed by the king's soldiers, and people who sheltered outlaws were outlawed themselves.

▲ In medieval China, a cangue was used as a punishment for assault. Standing with a heavy cangue around the neck was extremely tiring.

▼ Kings sometimes banished nobles for treason. Conspiring to overthrow the king was considered an act of treason.

Blood Feuds

In the early Middle Ages, the family of someone who had been injured or killed declared a private war, called a blood feud, on the person who had committed the crime and on that person's family. The feud continued for weeks or even years, until the victim's family felt the crime had been properly punished.

Kings and nobles tried to encourage other ways to resolve disputes. Sometimes, the criminal was forced to pay a *bot*, or fine, to the victim or to the victim's family. The fine for murder, called a *wergild*, was determined by the status of the person who had been killed. People who killed nobles were forced to pay a higher *wergild* than people who killed peasants.

Hangings and Beheadings

The accidental killing of a person, called manslaughter, and the intentional killing of a person, called murder, were less common crimes than assault. Men and women found guilty of manslaughter and murder were fined, hanged, or beheaded.

Day of Death

Hangings took place on a scaffold in a public square. The criminal stood on a block while a hangman placed a noose, or knotted rope, around the criminal's neck. Then, the hangman kicked the block away, and the person died quickly of a broken neck. In a beheading, a criminal knelt down with his head on a wooden block before him. Using an ax or sword, an executioner quickly chopped off the prisoner's head.

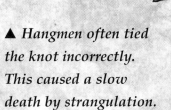

▲ *Hangmen often tied the knot incorrectly. This caused a slow death by strangulation.*

▶ *If done properly, a beheading was a quick and painless way to die, and was considered a more dignified death than hanging. For this reason, nobles sentenced to death were usually beheaded.*

Drawing and Quartering

Treason is the act of betraying, or acting against, one's country or ruler. This includes trying to kill the king or queen, kidnapping members of the royal family, or declaring war against the ruler.

In the Middle Ages, treason was considered one of the worst crimes. Traitors were usually drawn, or dragged behind a horse, to the public square where they were hanged. Before they were dead, they were taken down from the scaffold, their hearts and stomachs were cut out, and their bodies were quartered, or cut into four pieces. Sometimes, a criminal's remains were left on display to warn others about the cost of committing treason.

▼ *Medieval people often followed behind prisoners who were being drawn to their place of execution. At the public square they were joined by others to watch the criminals die.*

Punishment in Medieval Japan

Medieval Europe was not the only place where those found guilty of crimes were executed. In medieval Japan, criminals were quartered, impaled, or pierced with swords, boiled alive, or beheaded with metal saws. One of the most horrific methods of execution was being strung up. Criminals were tied to wooden frames with their arms stretched wide apart. Then, using spears, two executioners pierced the criminals' bodies several times. Finally, an executioner cut the criminals' necks, ensuring death.

Law Keepers

On every manor and in every town, there were people responsible for keeping law and order. On manors, bailiffs ensured that villagers paid their rents and fees, and they sometimes guarded suspected criminals until they were brought to court.

The Constable

Village constables settled disputes between peasants and arrested criminals. Special constables, called chief constables, lived in castles. They were responsible for suppressing, or putting an end to, riots and for gathering men to join the armies of the lord.

Tithings

In England, boys over the age of 12 were placed in groups of ten called tithings. Each member of a tithing made sure that the others obeyed the law. If a member of a tithing broke the law, the other members presented his crime to the manor court. Members of a tithing were also responsible for promising the court that the lawbreaker would pay off his debt or carry out his punishment. If the lawbreaker refused to pay his fine or debt, members of the tithing were sometimes forced to pay it for him.

▼ *On English manors, bailiffs oversaw the lords' crops and made sure that villagers did the work they owed their lords.*

◄ *Inspectors made sure that merchants measured goods accurately, that townspeople did not build additions to their homes that blocked city streets, and that citizens did not pollute the drinking water.*

► *The sheriff was an English law official who collected taxes and debts owed to the king. He also investigated crimes, arrested suspects, and sometimes judged court cases.*

The Hue and Cry

The hue and cry was a type of medieval alarm, used when a crime was committed on the manor. When someone's house was broken into, or when a person was assaulted, he or she yelled for help, or raised the hue and cry.

Everyone who heard the call was expected to try to capture the criminal and turn him over to the constable, bailiff, or another village official. The official kept the criminal in custody until the next manor or king's court was held. Those who did not respond to the hue and cry were sometimes fined.

Town Law Officials

Many different townspeople were paid to protect citizens and uphold the law. Most keepers of the law were honest and fair, but some drank in taverns when they were supposed to be working, and stole from merchants they were supposed to protect.

◄ *Night watchmen made sure that people stayed off the streets after curfew, ensured that prisoners did not escape, and called out if they saw a fire.*

► *Coroners investigated accidental or suspicious deaths by examining bodies for signs of violence and questioning witnesses.*

Medieval Prisons

I n the Middle Ages, people were not sent to prison as punishment for their crimes. Instead, prisons held those accused of crimes until their trials were held. Only people who owed large sums of money remained in prison after their trials. They were held until their families paid off their debts.

▲ *Bailiffs or guards, called goalers, escorted prisoners to court.*

Prisons and Goalers

Many prisons were located within the walls of the king's castle. They were often built underground out of dirt or stone, and had trap doors in their ceilings to let prisoners in or out. Goalers slept on the trap doors at night and put heavy boulders on them during the day so that prisoners could not escape.

Other prisons were in the high towers of castles. Tower prisons were not as damp and moldy as those underground, but they were just as uncomfortable. Wind, rain, and snow often came in through the windows, making the prisoners cold and wet.

▲ *Prisons built underground had few windows and were very dark, even in daytime.*

Prison Conditions

Conditions in prison varied, depending on a person's wealth. Prisoners had to purchase their own food, drink, clothes, blankets, beds, and firewood. Peasants who could not afford these items slept on bare stone or dirt floors, and often died from starvation and cold before their cases went to trial. Wealthy prisoners, who could afford to buy the supplies they needed, were more comfortable and had a much greater chance of surviving their time in prison.

▲ *Some nobles and kings were captured by their enemies and held for ransom. They were not allowed to go home until their families had paid money for their release.*

Prison Escapes

Goalers placed prisoners who they thought might escape in leg irons. Leg irons are heavy iron rings that are wrapped around a prisoner's ankles and attached to a floor or wall. A prisoner wearing leg irons is well restrained and cannot move very far.

Even though goalers guarded prisoners closely, some managed to escape. In April 1310, seven prisoners escaped from the jail in the southern French city of Toulouse. Prisoners held underground tunneled through the dirt behind the prison walls. Prisoners held above ground escaped by climbing down bed sheets tied together to make a rope.

▶ *Many prisoners made daring escapes.* The Historia Anglorum, *or* History of the English People, *describes how one prisoner in the heavily guarded Tower of London escaped into the Thames River after climbing down a ladder he had made out of bed sheets.*

23

Peasants' Courts

Disputes between peasants, and between peasants and the lord, were resolved in manor courts. Manor courts also tried cases in which peasants were accused of refusing to pay taxes, letting their animals run loose in the churchyard, and committing crimes, such as theft.

Manor Courts

Manor courts were held at least twice a year, and were presided over by the steward. The steward was chosen by the lord to supervise the manor. The steward gathered the villagers together in the lord's hall or in the village square. He appointed a jury of 12 men to tell the court about crimes that had been committed on the manor since the last manor court. Then, the jury decided on punishments and fines for villagers found guilty of breaking the law. If an accused person did not agree with the jury's verdict, or decision, he or she appealed to the villagers assembled at the court. If the entire community agreed with the verdict, the criminal was punished. If the community did not agree with the verdict, the criminal was not punished.

◄ *Town halls were medieval centers of government. In meeting rooms, the mayor and councilors discussed new laws, and held town court.*

Town Courts

In town courts, people were tried for crimes that included theft, slander, property damage, and assaults that were not violent, such as spitting on someone. Town courts met frequently, and were usually held in town halls. In the town court, a jury of citizens described crimes that had been committed to the judges. The accused were given the chance to defend themselves or, if they could afford it, to have a lawyer defend them. After all the evidence and arguments were heard, the mayor and his councilors voted on whether the accused was innocent or guilty. The verdict and punishment were then announced by the mayor.

◄ *Town councilors were either elected by citizens or were appointed by the king, nobles, or important townspeople.*

Ordeals

For much of the Middle Ages, cases were not tried in court before a judge and jury. Instead, people proved their innocence, or were found guilty, through tests called ordeals. Ordeals were based on the idea that God would protect the innocent and punish the guilty.

In ordeals by fire, people accused of crimes carried pieces of burning hot iron or walked on hot coals for a short time. If the wounds from their burns healed cleanly, they were judged innocent. In ordeals by hot water, the accused put their arms in very hot water. If their arms came out unharmed, they were declared innocent. In ordeals by cold water, suspects were completely immersed in a pool or stream. If they floated, they were believed to be guilty, as if the water had rejected them. There were also ordeals by combat, in which the accused fought accusers in duels.

◄ *People sometimes underwent ordeals on behalf of someone else. Here, a noblewoman proves the innocence of her husband in a trial by fire, holding a hot iron bar without injuring her hand.*

The King's Court

Violent crimes such as assault, murder, and treason were considered crimes against the king since they broke peace in the land that he ruled. These crimes were tried in a special court, called the king's court, which met several times a year.

People accused of crimes were tried by judges, who oversaw the courts, or by juries. At the beginning of trials, juries also described what they knew about the accused.

The sheriff brought prisoners from the prison to the court.

The court bailiff helped guard prisoners in court.

By the 1200s, lawyers represented wealthier people in court, especially those accused of serious crimes.

The person accused of a crime stood at a bar opposite the judges during the trial.

A notary kept a written record of the court proceedings for the king.

The king's court took place in town halls or in the halls of kings' castles.

The jury consisted of 12 to 24 prominent men from the town or from manors in the area.

Oathswearers were people who swore to an accused person's innocence. Five oathswearers were required for serious assaults, and 11 were needed for very serious crimes, such as murder.

Judges in the king's court were professionals who were trained in the law.

Church Courts

People convicted of moral crimes, such as holding beliefs that went against Christian teachings, gambling, and dancing in the churchyard, were tried in Church courts. Church courts also tried priests and other members of the clergy for crimes they were accused of committing.

Bishop-Judges

Church courts were led by **bishops** and their officials. They traveled throughout a diocese, the area over which a bishop had authority. In church courts, a jury was asked about moral crimes that had been committed in the area. The bishop and his officials heard each case, determined a person's guilt or innocence, and decided on the punishment.

Penance and Pilgrimages

For crimes such as gambling, people had to do penance, an act that showed they were sorry for what they had done. Penance included saying prayers over and over and fasting, or eating only bread and drinking only water, for several days. People accused of holding beliefs that went against the Church's teachings were sent on pilgrimages. Pilgrimages are religious journeys to holy places. Going on a pilgrimage was time-consuming and expensive. Many people were forced into debt to pay for food and supplies for the long journey.

◀ *In 1440, a Church court convicted a French noble named Gilles de Rais of* heresy *and excommunicated him. A judge of the king's court sentenced him to a beheading for committing multiple murders.*

EGIDII DE RAIZ
MILITIS PROCESSVS
IN FORO
ECCLESIASTICO
ANNO 1440

Crimes by Clergy

Priests, monks, and nuns who committed crimes such as theft or murder were tried in Church courts. Punishments were lighter than those in other courts. Punishment for theft was often fasting or doing penance, and punishment for murder was often a long pilgrimage.

People who did not belong to the clergy envied these lighter punishments, and many pretended to be priests, monks, and nuns so they could be tried in Church courts. Those who claimed to be members of the clergy had to read a passage from the Bible, the Christian holy book, as a test. If they passed the test, their case was heard by the bishop or his official.

▲ *Popes issued papal bulls when they decided upon new laws. Papal bulls were letters sealed with the pope's special seal, called a bulla.*

Excommunication

Church courts sometimes imposed physical punishments, such as beatings, the stocks, or the pillory. The most severe punishment that a Church court imposed was excommunication. Excommunication meant that people were not allowed to participate in Church rituals, such as **Mass**, **confession**, and marriage, until they were forgiven by Church officials for their crimes. Some people who were excommunicated were also forced to leave their homes, and were banished from society.

▼ *In 1095, Pope Urban II excommunicated King Philip I of France for trying to divorce his wife. Divorce was not allowed by the Catholic Church.*

Inquisitions

Inquisitions were special kinds of Church courts. They were created in 1233 and continued, in different forms, until the 1800s. Inquisitions dealt with a crime called heresy, in people were accused of holding religious beliefs that went against the Church's teachings. These people were called heretics

Medieval people believed that heretics angered God and endangered the rest of society. They thought that God might destroy a village's crops, bring disease, or even destroy an entire town because a heretic lived there.

Inquisitorial Courts

In Inquisitions, judges called inquisitors heard **testimonies** from members of the community about suspected heretics. Then, they questioned suspects in court. If suspected heretics could prove that they were true Christians by answering questions about Christian teachings, they were released. If they did not answer correctly, they were considered heretics, and were asked to confess.

Catharism

In the Middle Ages, the most common type of heresy was Catharism. Cathar heretics believed that there were two gods, a good god who ruled the spiritual world of angels, and an evil god who ruled the everyday world where people lived. This went against the Christian teaching that there is only one God. Cathars also did not believe that priests were required to perform marriages, hear confessions, or say Mass.

▶ *A legend tells of Saint Dominic, who fought against the Cathars, and a great Cathar scholar whi each wrote a book to defend their religious beliefs. Judges threw both books into a fire. When Dominic's book leapt out of the flames, they were convinced that the teachings it contained were correct.*

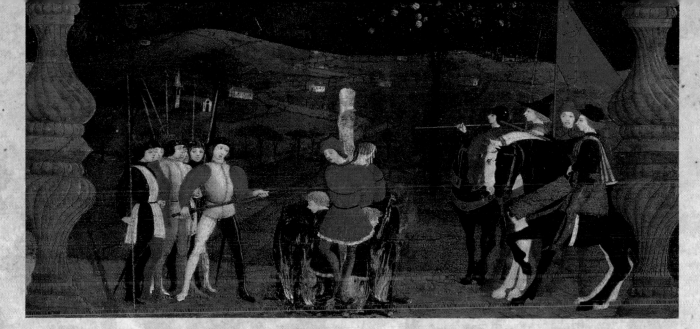

Torture

Suspects who confessed to their crimes had to do penance. Those who did not confess were imprisoned and tortured until they admitted that they had sinned. They were not allowed to sleep, and were whipped or beaten. Some had burning hot cooking fat applied to the soles of their feet, while others were tortured with a device called a strappado. In the strappado, heretics' hands were tied behind their backs, and they were hoisted off the ground with pulleys attached to their wrists. Then, they were dropped partway to the ground with a jerk that caused a great deal of pain, and sometimes dislocated their shoulders.

▲ *Heretics who refused to confess, or who confessed but continued to defend their beliefs after their release from prison, were burned at the stake.*

The Spanish Inquisition

In 1478, King Ferdinand and Queen Isabella of Spain founded the Spanish Inquisition to punish **Jews** and **Muslims** who had **converted** to Christianity but continued to follow the laws and practices of their old religions in secret. Queen Isabella believed that Jews and Muslims who pretended to be Christian to avoid persecution, or cruel treatment, would cause Christians to change their beliefs. After 1500, the Spanish Inquisition also tried suspected heretics and witches, who were thought to threaten Christian teachings and practices.

▶ *During the Spanish Inquisition, Jews and Muslims found guilty of practicing their religions in secret confessed their crimes and heard their punishments at special ceremonies called autos-da-fés, or "acts of faith."*

Glossary

assault A physical attack on another person or a person's property

banish To force someone to leave the place where he or she lives

bishop A high-ranking religious leader in the Catholic Church

blacksmith A person who makes tools from iron

Byzantine Relating to an empire once located in what is now Greece and Turkey

Christianity The religion that follows the teachings of God and of Jesus Christ, who Christians believe is God's son

confession A declaration of one's sins to a priest

convert To adopt a different religion, faith, or belief

duel To fight another person, often with a sword

empire A group of countries or territories under one ruler or government

execute To kill someone as punishment

famine An extreme shortage of food that causes many people to go hungry

grindstone A large stone wheel used for grinding grain into flour

heresy A belief that goes against the teachings of the Church

Jew A person whose religion is Judaism. Jewish people believe in one God and follow the teachings of a holy book called the *Torah*

Mass The main ceremony of the Roman Catholic Church

monk A male member of a religious community who devotes his life to prayer, work, and study

moral Relating to the idea of what is right and wrong

Muslim Belonging to the religion of Islam. Muslims believe in one God, called Allah, and follow the teachings of his prophet Muhammad

nun A female member of a religious community who devotes her life to prayer, work, and study

outlaw A criminal who is banished from a community and loses all legal rights

overthrow To remove from power, often by force

pillory A device used for punishment, consisting of a wooden frame in which a criminal's hands and feet are locked

Roman An ancient people, based in Rome, who ruled a large empire from about 100 B.C. to 400 A.D.

sheriff A law enforcement officer

slander The act of making false or damaging statements about another person

testimony A statement provided by a witness as evidence

treason The act of betraying, or acting against, one's country or ruler

Index

1 2 3 4 5 6 7 8 9 0 Printed in the U.S.A. 0 9 8 7 6 5 4